What Every Child Should Know - Kindergarten and First Grade.

TASK INCLUDE:
- Alphabets
- Numbers
- Colors & Shapes
- Money Identification
- Mathematics
- Phonics
- Spelling Word Families
- Simple Punctuation &
- Capitalization
- Telling Time
- ...and more

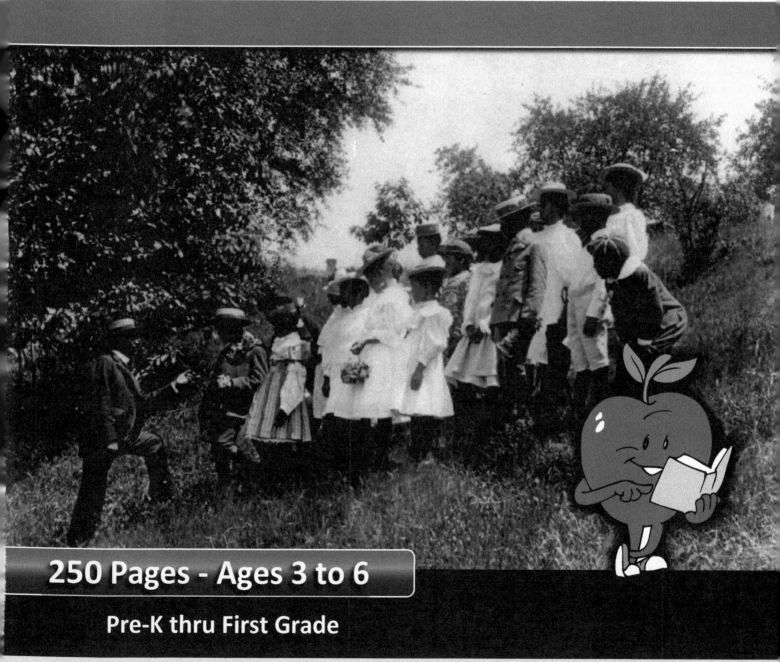

250 Pages - Ages 3 to 6

Pre-K thru First Grade

© 12 Tribes Publishing
Designed and produced by
12 Tribes Publishing
United States

Published in the United States
in 2016

Editors: 12 Tribes Network Staff

Printed in The United States

ISBN: 978-1-365-35531-8
All rights reserved

What every child should know for preschool, kindergarten and first grade. Hebrew Lessons Included.

12 Tribes Publishing
United States

CONTENTS

Alphabets, Uppercase and Lowercase 6-36

Learning Shapes 37-49

Learning Colors...50-62

Learning Numbers and Counting 63-77

Learning Directions 78-84

Learning Perception .... 85 -133

Identifying Coins 134-142

Perception Test 143-148

Hard or Soft?...149-151

Bigger or Smaller?..152-156

Cutout and Match...157-172

What Time is it?...169-174

Small Sentences A - Z..175-176

Words to Know 177-179

Addition and Subtraction, Single & Double Digit no Regrouping 180-187

Phonics 188-192

Spelling Word Families and Word Play 193-201

Prepositions and Conjunctions 202-203

Show an Opinion 204

Practice Writing and Tracing 205-208

Paleo Hebrew Alphabet..209-232

Tribes of Israel (Yisrael) worksheets..233-244

Terms for Kinship...245-250

Introduction

Children are fast learners naturally, so having a good variety of things to learn at an early age can give them the head start they need. This publication was designed to grow with your preschooler and carry them into first grade with ease.

They will learn words as they learn their alphabets and numbers, they will learn how to identify colors and shapes along with word association, they will learn perception and directions, time in both digital and analog, math, simple grammar and much more.

All subjects included in this publication were specifically designed to maximize each student's learning. We have included more than one level of learning for each topic to strengthen their comprehension.

Name_____

Learning Alphabets With Words

Color the picture and trace the word.

Aa

Ant

Ant

Name_____

Learning Alphabets With Words

Color the picture and trace the word.

Bb

Bird

Name_____

Learning Alphabets With Words

Cc

Color the picture and trace the word.

Cat

_ _
Cat
_ _

Name_____

Learning Alphabets With Words

Color the picture and trace the word.

Dd

Dog

9

Name_____

Learning Alphabets With Words

Color the picture and trace the word.

Ee

Eagle

Eagle

Name_____

Learning Alphabets With Words

Color the picture and trace the word.

Ff

Fish

Fish

11

Name_____

Learning Alphabets With Words

Color the picture and trace the word.

Gg

Goat

12

Name_____

Learning Alphabets With Words

Color the picture and trace the word.

Hh

Horse

13

Name_____

Learning Alphabets With Words

Color the picture and trace the word.

Insect

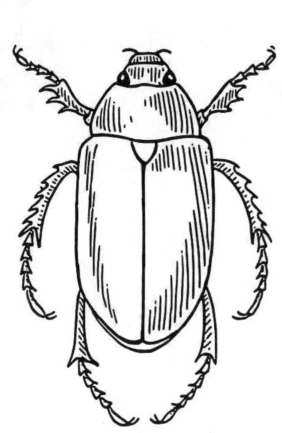

Insect

14

Name_____

Learning Alphabets With Words

Color the picture and trace the word.

Jj

Jellyfish

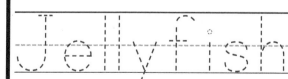

15

Name_____

Learning Alphabets With Words

Color the picture and trace the word.

Kk

Kangaroo

Kangaroo

Name_____

Learning Alphabets With Words

Color the picture and trace the word.

Ll

Lion

Name_____

Learning Alphabets With Words

Color the picture and trace the word.

Mm

Monkey

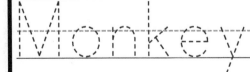

18

Name_____

Learning Alphabets With Words

Color the picture and trace the word.

Nn

Newt

Newt

Name_____

Learning Alphabets With Words

Color the picture and trace the word.

Oo

Otter

Otter

20

Name_____

Learning Alphabets With Words

Color the picture and trace the word.

Pp   Possum

Possum

Name_____

Learning Alphabets With Words

Color the picture and trace the word.

Qq

Quail

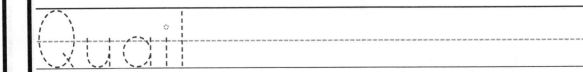

Quail

22

Name_____

Learning Alphabets With Words

Color the picture and trace the word.

Rr

Rabbit

Rabbit

Name_____

Learning Alphabets With Words

Color the picture and trace the word.

Ss

Seal

Name_____

Learning Alphabets With Words

Color the picture and trace the word.

Tt

Tiger

Name_____

Learning Alphabets With Words

Color the picture and trace the word.

Uu

Umbrella Bird

‧‧Umbrella Bird‧‧

Name_____

Learning Alphabets With Words

Color the picture and trace the word.

Vv

Vulture

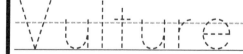

27

Name_____

Learning Alphabets With Words

Color the picture and trace the word.

Ww

Whale

Whale

Name_____

Learning Alphabets With Words

Color the picture and trace the word.

X-Ray Tetra

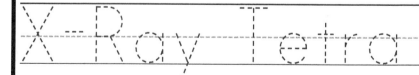

Name_____

Learning Alphabets With Words

Color the picture and trace the word.

Yy

Yak

Yak _____

30

Name_____

Learning Alphabets With Words

Color the picture and trace the word.

Zz

Zebra

Zebra

Name_____

Match Uppercase with Lowercase Letters

A		d
B		b
C		f
D		a
E		g
F		e
G		c

Aa	Bb	Cc	Dd	Ee	Ff
Gg	Hh	Ii	Jj	Kk	Ll
Mm	Nn	Oo	Pp	Qq	Rr
Ss	Tt	Uu	Vv	Ww	Xx
Yy	Zz				

UPPER CASE & lower case
Alphabets

Name_____

Match Uppercase With Lowercase Letters

H		j
I		k
J		h
K		m
L		i
M		n
N		l

Name_____

Match Uppercase With Lowercase Letters

V		x
W		z
X		v
Y		y
Z		w

Name_____

Match Uppercase With Lowercase Letters

O			q
P			s
Q			u
R			o
S			r
T			p
U			t

36

Name_____

Learning Your Shapes

Color the shape and trace the word.

Circle

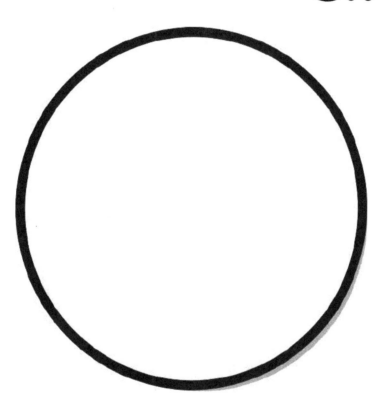

Name_____

Learning Your Shapes

Color the shape and trace the word.

Square

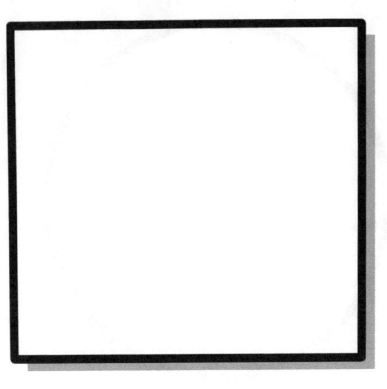

Name_____

Learning Your Shapes

Color the shape and trace the word.

Triangle

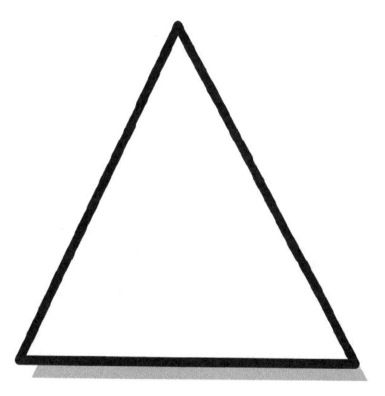

Name_____

Learning Your Shapes

Color the shape and trace the word.

Rectangle

40

Name_____

Learning Your Shapes

Color the shape and trace the word.

Trapezoid

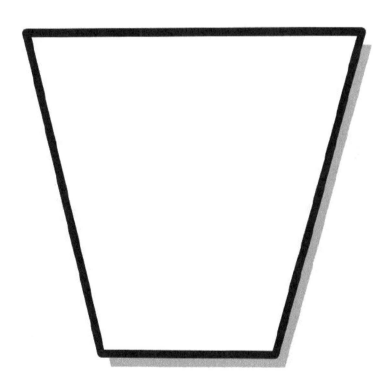

Name_____

Learning Your Shapes

Color the shape and trace the word.

Diamond

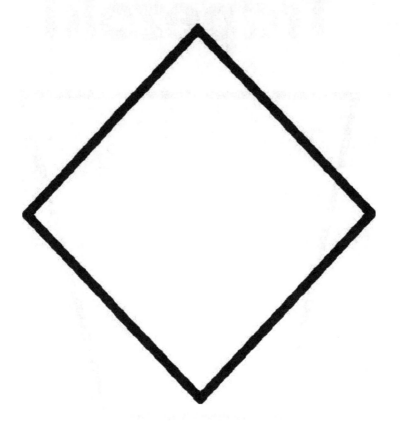

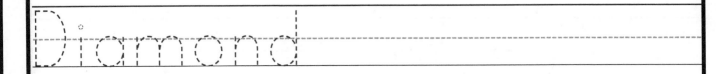

Name_____

Learning Your Shapes

Color the shape and trace the word.

Heart

Heart

43

Name_____

Learning Your Shapes

Color the shape and trace the word.

Cylinder

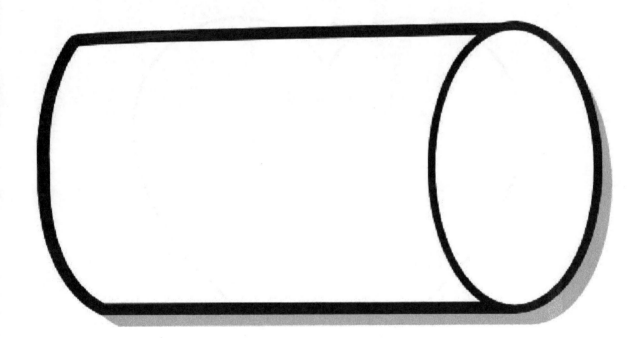

Cylinder

Name_____

Learning Your Shapes

Color the shape and trace the word.

Cube

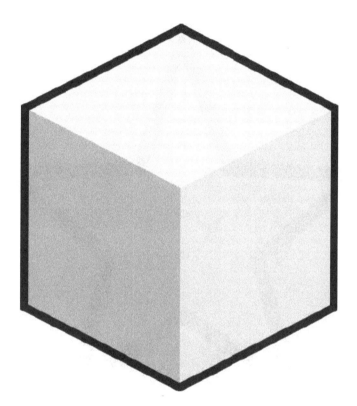

Name_____

Learning Your Shapes

Color the shape and trace the word.

Star

Star

Name_____

Learning Your Shapes

Color the shape and trace the word.

Moon

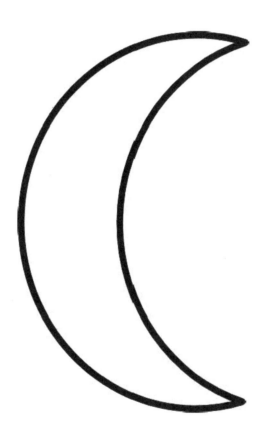

Moon

Shapes

Directions: Write the correct name for each shape on the lines provided.

Star - Octagon - Hexagon - Trapezoid - Pentagon Square - Circle - Rectangle - Triangle - Oval

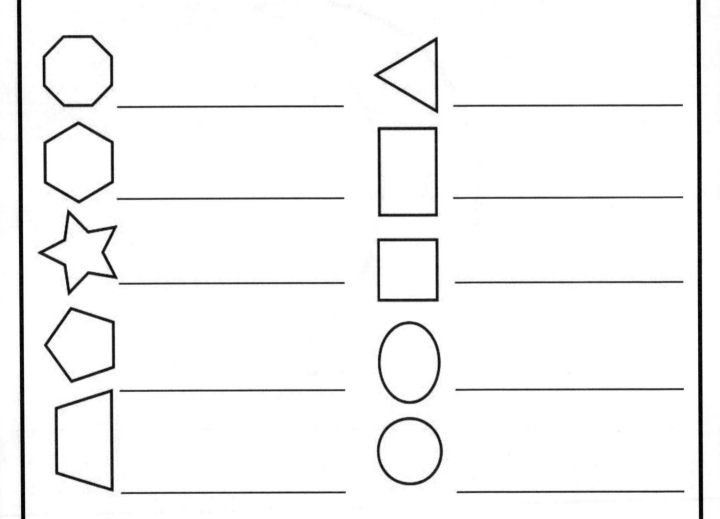

Directions: Put an X next to the word whose shape in not shown on the right.

Color the <u>circle</u> red, color the <u>square</u> blue, color the <u>star</u> yellow, color the <u>rectangle</u> orange and color the <u>oval</u> black.

circle
square
triangle
rectangle
diamond

49

Name_____

Learning Your Colors

Spell each word out loud and trace the word below.

Red

50

Name_____

Learning Your Colors

Spell each word out loud and trace the word below.

Blue

Blue

Blue

Blue

Name_____

Learning Your Colors

Spell each word out loud and trace the word below.

Yellow

Yellow

Yellow

Name_____

Learning Your Colors

Spell each word out loud and trace the word below.

Green

Green

Green

Green

Name_____

Learning Your Colors

Spell each word out loud and trace the word below.

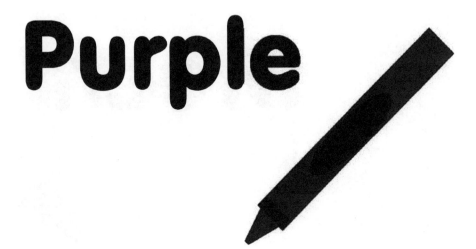

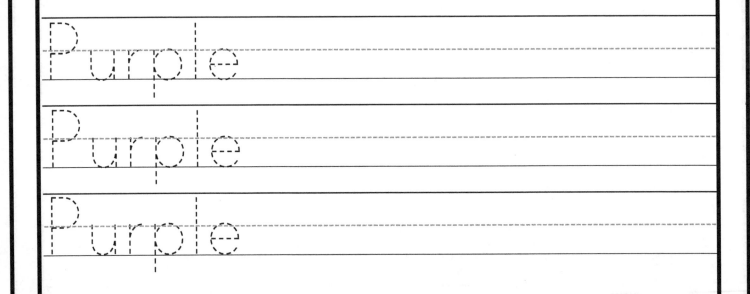

Name_____

Learning Your Colors

Spell each word out loud and trace the word below.

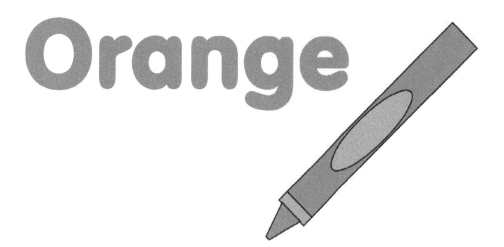

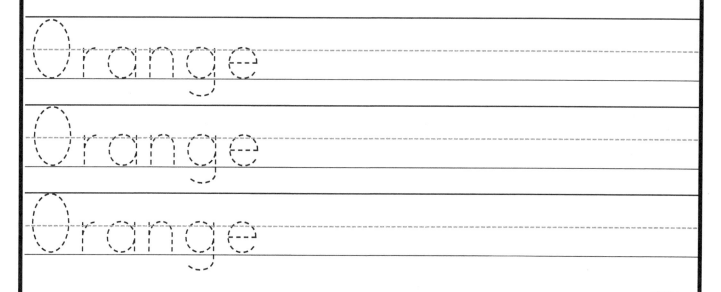

Name_____

Learning Your Colors

Spell each word out loud and trace the word below.

Pink

Pink

Pink

Pink

Name_____

Learning Your Colors
Spell each word out loud and trace the word below.

Brown

Brown

Brown

Brown

Name_____

Learning Your Colors

Spell each word out loud and trace the word below.

Black

Name_____

Learning Your Numbers

Spell each word out loud, say the number and trace the word below.

Zero 0

Name_____

Learning Your Numbers

Spell each word out loud, say the number and trace the word below.

One

Name_____

Learning Your Numbers

Spell each word out loud, say the number and trace the word below.

Two

Name_____

Learning Your Numbers

Spell each word out loud, say the number and trace the word below.

Three 3

Name_____

Learning Your Numbers
Spell each word out loud, say the number and trace the word below.

Four 4

4   4

4   4

Four

63

Name_____

Learning Your Numbers

Spell each word out loud, say the number and trace the word below.

5 5

5 5

Five

Name_____

Learning Your Numbers

Spell each word out loud, say the number and trace the word below.

Six

65

Name_____

Learning Your Numbers

Spell each word out loud, say the number and trace the word below.

Seven

Name_____

Learning Your Numbers

Spell each word out loud, say the number and trace the word below.

Name_____

Learning Your Numbers

Spell each word out loud, say the number and trace the word below.

9 9

9 9

Nine

Name_____

Learning Your Numbers

Spell each word out loud, say the number and trace the word below.

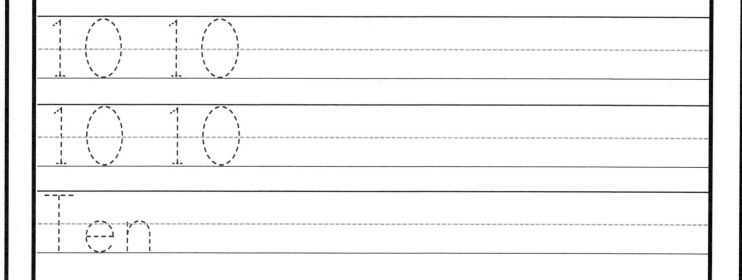

69

How Many Dots are on the Domino?

Count the dots on each domino and record the number below.

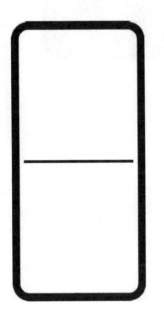
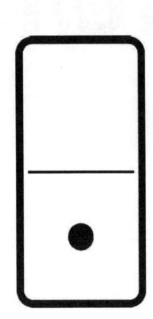
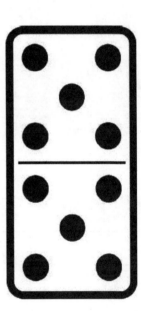

Name_____

How Many Dots are on the Domino?

Count the dots on each domino and record the number below.

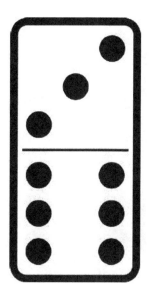 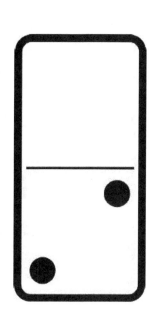 

Name_____

How Many Dots are on the Domino?

Count the dots on each domino and record the number below.

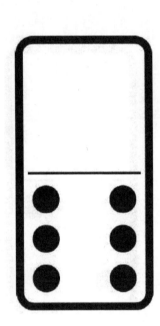
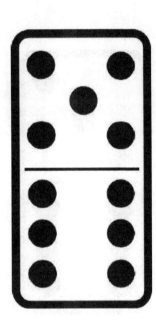

Name_____

How Many Dots are on the Domino?

Count the dots on each domino and record the number below.

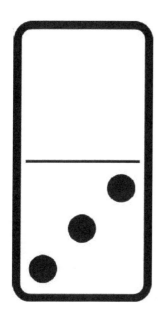 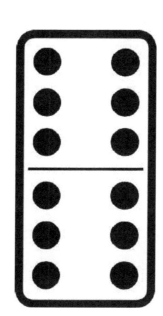 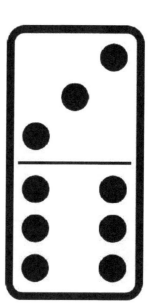

Name_____

Learning Directions With Arrows

Spell each word out loud, say the direction and trace the word below.

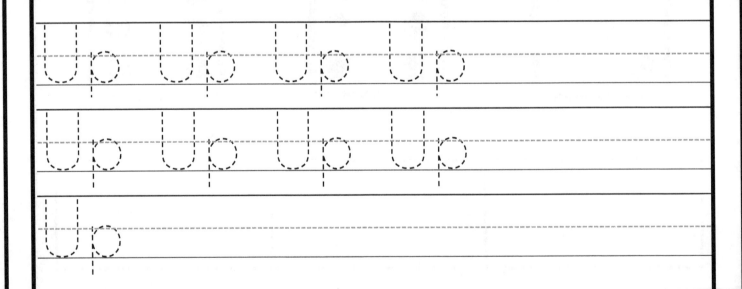

Name_____

Learning Directions With Arrows

Spell each word out loud, say the direction and trace the word below.

Down

Down Down

Down Down

Down

Name_____

Learning Directions With Arrows

Spell each word out loud, say the direction and trace the word below.

Right

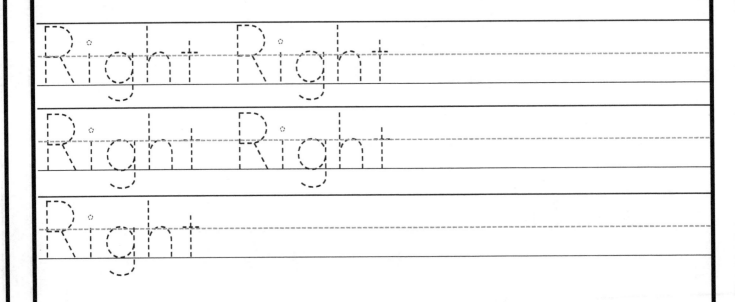

Name_____

Learning Directions With Arrows

Spell each word out loud, say the direction and trace the word below.

Left

Left Left Left

Left Left Left

Left

77

Name_____

Learning Directions With Arrows

Write the word "Right" in the arrow that's pointing right. Write the word "Left" in the arrow that's pointing left. Write the word "Up" in the arrow that's pointing upward. Write the word "Down" in the arrow that's pointing downward.

Name_____

Learning Directions With Arrows

Spell each word out loud, say the direction and trace the word below.

In

in in in in in in in

In in in in in in in

In

Name_____

Learning Directions With Arrows

Spell each word out loud, say the direction and trace the word below.

Out

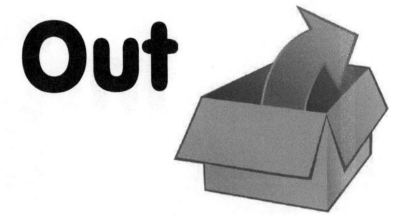

Out out out out

Out out out out

Out

Name_____

Learning Perception

Spell each word out loud, describe what you see and trace the word below.

Open

Open open

Open open

Open

Name_____

Learning Perception

Spell each word out loud, describe what you see and trace the word below.

Shut

Shut shut shut shut
Shut shut shut
Shut

Name_____

Learning Perception

Spell each word out loud, describe what you see and trace the word below.

Empty

Empty empty

Empty empty

Empty

83

Name_____

Learning Perception

Spell each word out loud, describe what you see and trace the word below.

Full

Full full full full

Full full full full

Full

Name_____

Learning Perception

Spell each word out loud, describe what you see and trace the word below.

Circle the one that is off.

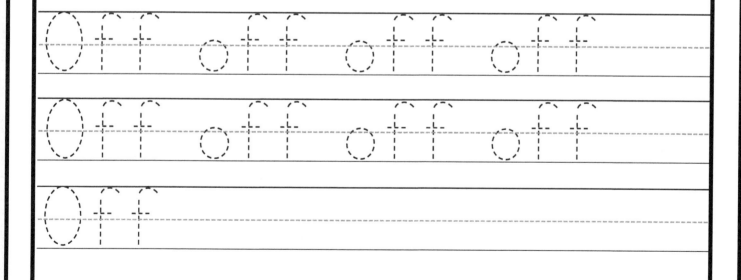

Name_____

Learning Perception

Spell each word out loud, describe what you see and trace the word below.

Circle the one that is off.

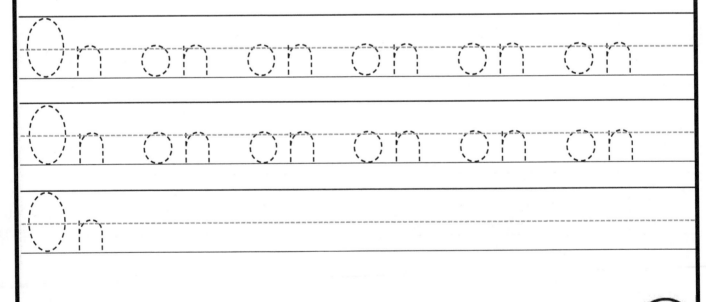

Name_____

Learning Perception

Spell each word out loud, describe what you see and trace the word below.

Apple

Apple apple

Apple apple

Apple

Name_____

Learning Perception

Spell each word out loud, describe what you see and trace the word below.

Banana

Banana banana

Banana banana

Banana

Name_____

Learning Perception

Spell each word out loud, describe what you see and trace the word below.

Butter

Butter butter

Butter butter

Butter

Name_____

Learning Perception

Spell each word out loud, describe what you see and trace the word below.

Bread

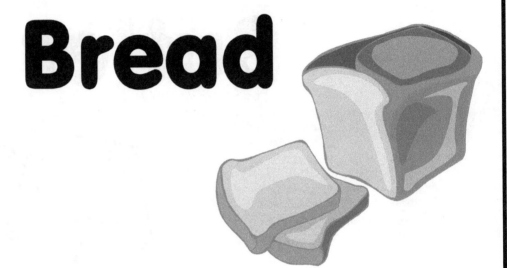

Bread bread

Bread bread

Bread

Name_____

Learning Perception

Spell each word out loud, describe what you see and trace the word below.

Carrot

Carrot carrot
Carrot carrot carrot
Carrot

Name_____

Learning Perception

Spell each word out loud, describe what you see and trace the word below.

Cake

Cake cake cake

Cake cake cake

Cake

Name_____

Learning Perception

Spell each word out loud, describe what you see and trace the word below.

Cherries

Cherries cherries

Cherries cherries

Cherries

Name_____

Learning Perception

Spell each word out loud, describe what you see and trace the word below.

Corn

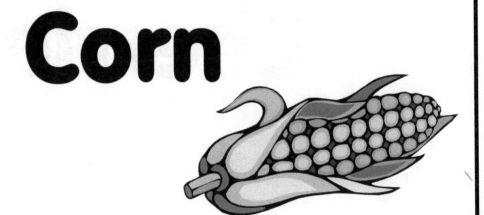

Corn corn corn corn

Corn corn corn corn

Corn

Name_____

Learning Perception

Spell each word out loud, describe what you see and trace the word below.

Eggs

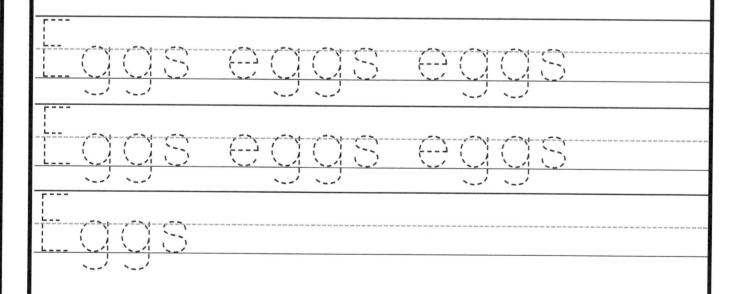

Name_____

Learning Perception

Spell each word out loud, describe what you see and trace the word below.

Fish

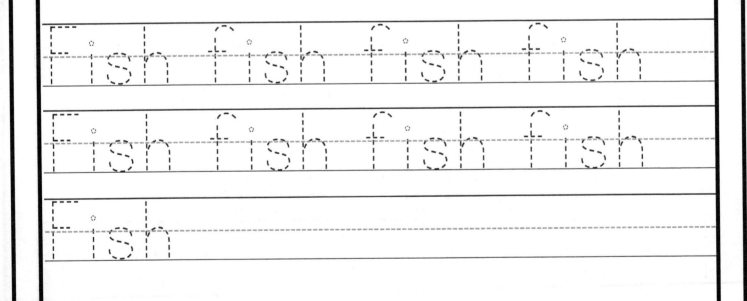

Name_____

Learning Perception

Spell each word out loud, describe what you see and trace the word below.

Grapes

Grapes grapes

Grapes grapes

Grapes

Name_____

Learning Perception

Spell each word out loud, describe what you see and trace the word below.

Lemon

`Lemon lemon lemon`

`Lemon lemon lemon`

`Lemon`

Name_____

Learning Perception

Spell each word out loud, describe what you see and trace the word below.

Lime

Lime lime lime lime

Lime lime lime lime

Lime

Name_____

Learning Perception

Spell each word out loud, describe what you see and trace the word below.

Milk

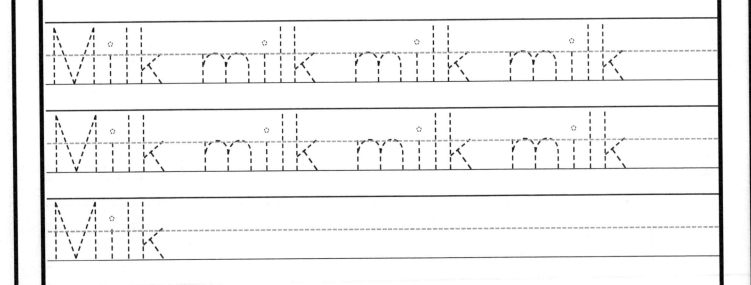

100

Name_____

Learning Perception

Spell each word out loud, describe what you see and trace the word below.

Kiwi

Kiwi Kiwi Kiwi Kiwi

Kiwi Kiwi Kiwi Kiwi

Kiwi

Name_____

Learning Perception

Spell each word out loud, describe what you see and trace the word below.

Muffin muffin

Muffin muffin

Muffin

Name_____

Learning Perception

Spell each word out loud, describe what you see and trace the word below.

Mushrooms

Mushrooms

Mushrooms

Mushrooms

Name_____

Learning Perception

Spell each word out loud, describe what you see and trace the word below.

Orange

Orange orange

Orange orange

Orange

Name_____

Learning Perception

Spell each word out loud, describe what you see and trace the word below.

Peanut

Peanut peanut

Peanut peanut

Peanut

Name_____

Learning Perception

Spell each word out loud, describe what you see and trace the word below.

Pear

Pear pear pear

Pear pear pear

Pear

Name_____

Learning Perception

Spell each word out loud, describe what you see and trace the word below.

Pineapple

Pineapple pineapple

Pineapple pineapple

Pineapple

Name_____

Learning Perception

Spell each word out loud, describe what you see and trace the word below.

Pretzel

Pretzel pretzel

Pretzel pretzel

Pretzel

Name_____

Learning Perception

Spell each word out loud, describe what you see and trace the word below.

Pumpkin

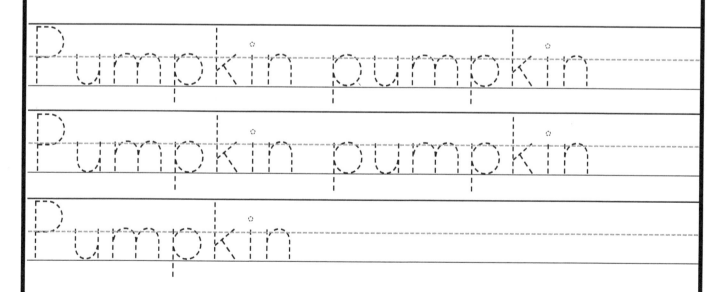

109

Name_____

Learning Perception

Spell each word out loud, describe what you see and trace the word below.

Strawberries

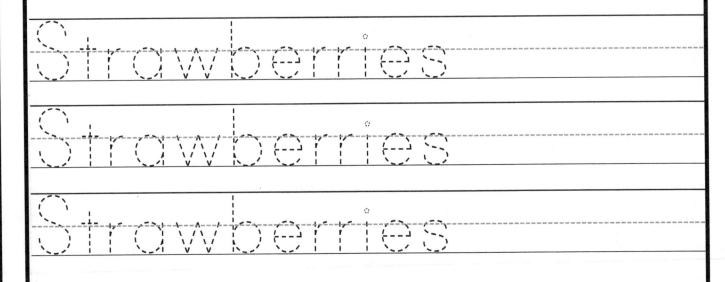

110

Name_____

Learning Perception

Spell each word out loud, describe what you see and trace the word below.

Watermelon

Watermelon

Watermelon

Watermelon

Name_____

Learning Perception

Spell each word out loud, describe what you see and trace the word below.

Tomato

Tomato tomato

Tomato tomato

Tomato

Name_____

Learning Perception

Spell each word out loud, describe what you see and trace the word below.

Coffee

Coffee coffee

Coffee coffee

Coffee

Name_____

Learning Perception

Spell each word out loud, describe what you see and trace the word below.

Shoes shoes shoes

Shoes shoes shoes

Shoes

Name_____

Learning Perception

Spell each word out loud, describe what you see and trace the word below.

Taco taco taco

Taco taco taco

Taco

115

Name_____

Learning Perception

Spell each word out loud, describe what you see and trace the word below.

Feet

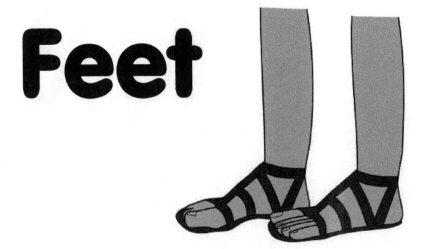

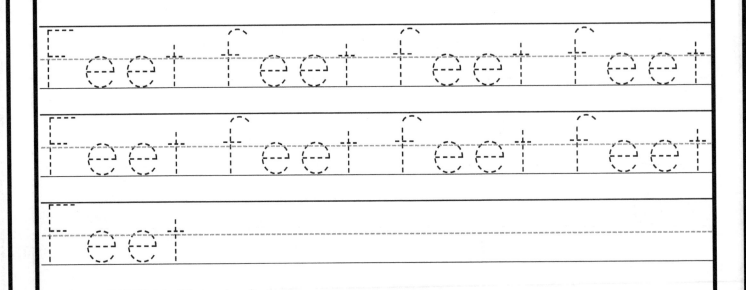

Name_____

Learning Perception

Spell each word out loud, describe what you see and trace the word below.

Bat

Bat bat bat bat bat

Bat bat bat bat bat

Bat

Name_____

Learning Perception

Spell each word out loud, describe what you see and trace the word below.

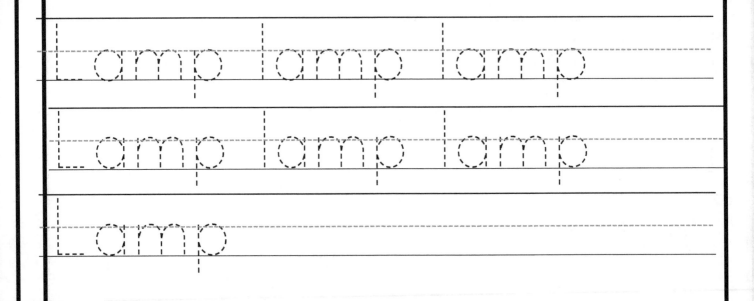

118

Name_____

Learning Perception

Spell each word out loud, describe what you see and trace the word below.

Ball

Ball ball ball ball ball

Ball ball ball ball ball

Ball

Name_____

Learning Perception

Spell each word out loud, describe what you see and trace the word below.

Table

Table table table

Table table table

Table

120

Name_____

Learning Perception

Spell each word out loud, describe what you see and trace the word below.

Tape

Tape tape tape

Tape tape tape

Tape

Name_____

Learning Perception

Spell each word out loud, describe what you see and trace the word below.

Asleep

Asleep asleep

Asleep asleep

Asleep

Name_____

Learning Perception

Spell each word out loud, describe what you see and trace the word below.

Awake

Awake awake

Awake awake

Awake

Name_____

Learning Perception

Spell each word out loud, describe what you see and trace the word below.

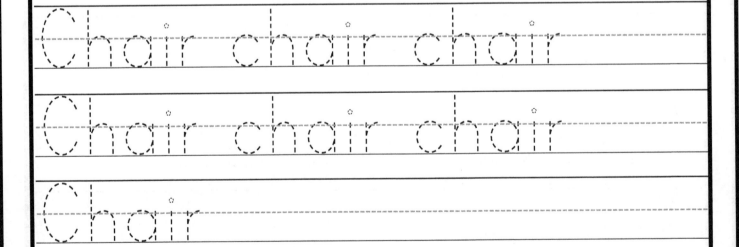

Name_____

Learning Perception

Spell each word out loud, describe what you see and trace the word below.

Fire

Fire fire fire fire

Fire fire fire fire

Fire

Name_____

Learning Perception

Spell each word out loud, describe what you see and trace the word below.

Shirt

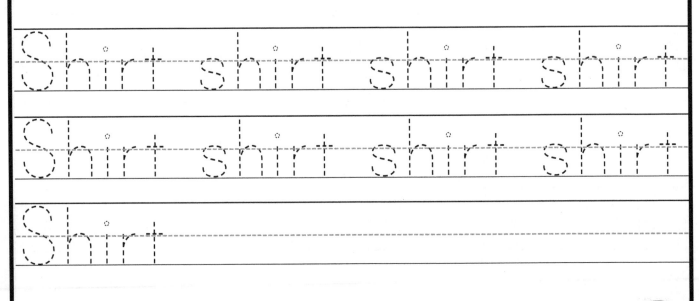

Name_____

Learning Perception

Spell each word out loud, describe what you see and trace the word below.

Family

Family family

Family family

Family

Name_____

Learning Perception

Spell each word out loud, describe what you see and trace the word below.

Sitting

Circle the one that's sitting

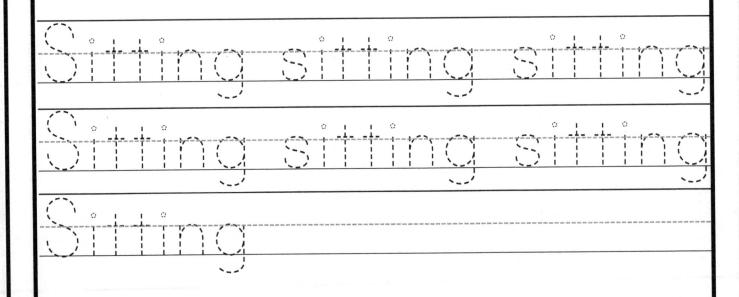

128

Name_____

Learning Perception

Spell each word out loud, describe what you see and trace the word below.

Standing

Circle the one that's standing

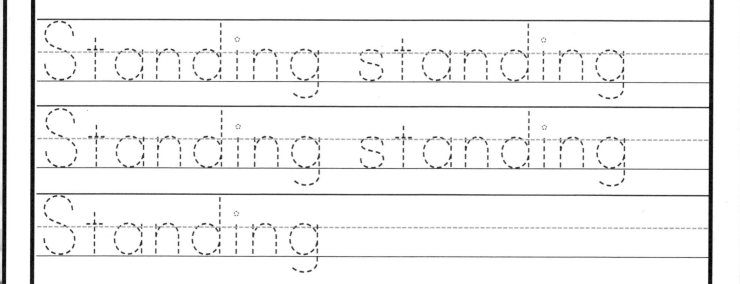

Name_____

Study Guide for Identifying Coins

Penny 1¢	*Dime* 10¢	*Nickel* 5¢	*Quarter* 25¢

Coin Name	Word Value	Number Value
Penny	One Cent	1¢
Dime	Ten Cents	10¢
Nickel	Five Cents	5¢
Quarter	Twenty Five Cents	25¢

130

Name_____

Identifying Coins

Spell each word out loud. Say the coin type out loud. Trace the word below.

Penny

Penny Penny Penny

Penny Penny Penny

Penny

Name_____

Counting Coins

How many coins do you see? Put your answer in the box below.

Penny

Name_____

Identifying Coins

Spell each word out loud. Say the coin type out loud. Trace the word below.

Nickel

Nickel nickel nickel

Nickel nickel nickel

Nickel

Name_____

Counting Coins

How many coins do you see? Put your answer in the box below.

Nickel

Name_____

Identifying Coins

Spell each word out loud. Say the coin type out loud. Trace the word below.

Dime

Name_____

Counting Coins

How many coins do you see? Put your answer in the box below.

Dime

Name_____

Identifying Coins

Spell each word out loud. Say the coin type out loud. Trace the word below.

Quarter

Quarter Quarter

Quarter Quarter

Quarter

Name_____

Counting Coins

How many coins do you see? Put your answer in the box below.

Quarter

Name_____

Perception Test

Directions: Draw an X through the word that doesn't belong.

Chair	Table
Lamp	Shovel

Rabbit	Dog
Cat	Fish

Shoe	Sock
Glove	Boat

Rock	Pebble
Leaf	Stone

Water	Ice
Milk	Juice

Lemon	Orange
Grapefruit	Apple

139

Name_____

Perception Test

Directions: Draw an X through the word that doesn't belong.

Paper	Pencil
Crayon	Marker

Shirt	Coat
Dress	Pants

Fly	Beetle
Bird	Knat

Red	Blue
Pink	Dry

Floor	Wall
Door	Tree

Car	Boat
Train	Truck

140

Name_____

Perception Test

Directions: Draw an X through the word that doesn't belong.

New	Up
Down	Left

Iron	Bike
Scooter	Tricycle

Sister	Pet
Brother	Cousin

Sky	Grass
Flower	Tree

Eye	Foot
Arm	Leg

Fork	Spoon
Blender	Knife

Name_____

Perception Test

Directions: Draw an X through the word that doesn't belong.

Pig	Cow
Horse	Tiger

Phone	Book
Radio	Ipad

Circle	Square
Coin	Triangle

Hat	Cap
Glove	Hood

Apple	Book
Aunt	Ant

Paint	Chalk
Pencil	Pen

142

Name_____

Perception Test

Directions: Draw an X through the word that doesn't belong.

Dad	Mom
Friend	Sister

Red	Yellow
Black	Rock

Moon	Stars
Bike	Sun

Grape	Ball
Orange	Table

Window	Door
Lamp	Wall

Up	Back
Down	Inside

143

Name_____

Perception Test

Directions: Draw a line to the word that describes each picture.

Crying   Laughing   Surprised

Name_____

Hard or Soft

Look at the images and determine if they are hard or soft to the touch.

Hard  **Soft**

Hard  **Soft**

Hard  **Soft**

Hard  **Soft**

Name_____

Hard or Soft

Look at the images and determine if they are hard or soft to the touch.

Hard  **Soft**

Hard  **Soft**

Hard  **Soft**

Hard 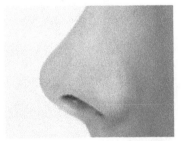 **Soft**

Name_____

Hard or Soft

Look at the images and determine if they are hard or soft to the touch.

Hard  **Soft**

Hard  **Soft**

Hard  **Soft**

Hard  **Soft**

147

Name_____

Bigger or Smaller

Which object is smaller?

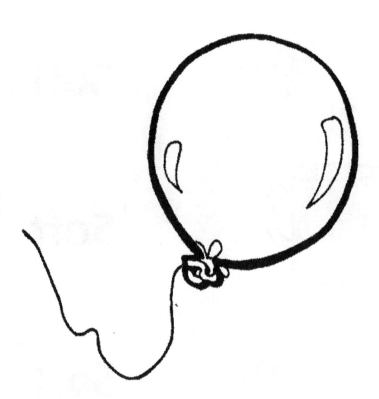
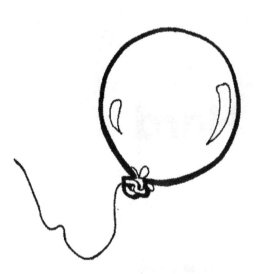

Smaller smaller

148

Name_____

Bigger or Smaller

Which object is smaller?

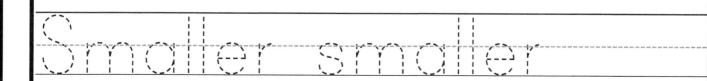

149

Name_____

Bigger or Smaller

Which object is bigger?

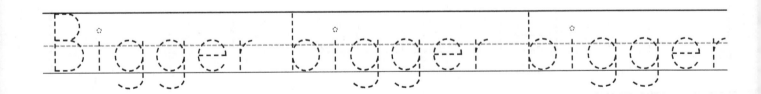

Name_____

Bigger or Smaller

Which object is bigger?

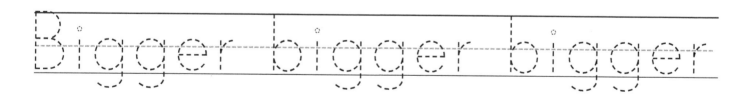

Name_____

Bigger or Smaller

Which object is bigger?

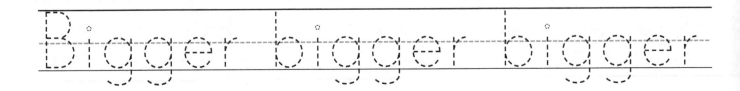

Cut out the word number cards and paste them on top of the correct number. Be sure to keep the number and word facing outward so that they can be seen when flipping your cards over.

one	3
two	2
three	5
four	1
five	4

Cut out the word number cards and paste them on top of the correct number. Be sure to keep the number and word facing outward so that they can be seen when flipping your cards over.

six	10
seven	8
eight	7
nine	6
ten	9

Cut out the opposites cards and paste them on top of the correct opposite word. Be sure to keep the words facing outward so that they can be seen when flipping your cards over.

up	out
back	under
in	down
black	white
over	front

Cut out the opposite cards and paste them on top of the correct opposite word. Be sure to keep the words facing outward so that they can be seen when flipping your cards over.

open	large
left	woman
small	girl
boy	shut
man	right

Cut out the opposite cards and paste them on top of the correct opposite word. Be sure to keep the words facing outward so that they can be seen when flipping your cards over.

good	cold
hot	bad
short	open
big	tall
close	little

Cut out the opposite cards and paste them on top of the correct opposite word. Be sure to keep the words facing outward so that they can be seen when flipping your cards over.

push	last
first	right
old	pull
wrong	old
young	new

Cut out the opposite cards and paste them on top of the correct opposite word. Be sure to keep the words facing outward so that they can be seen when flipping your cards over.

inside	smile
happy	cry
frown	sad
laugh	dad
mom	outside

Cut out the opposite cards and paste them on top of the correct opposite word. Be sure to keep the words facing outward so that they can be seen when flipping your cards over.

sister	low
cat	nice
high	dog
mean	hard
soft	brother

What Time Is It

What Time Is It?

The clock shows 1 o'clock.

What Time Is It?

The clock shows 1:30.

What Time Is It?

The clock shows 2 o'clock.

What Time Is It?

The clock shows 2:30.

What Time Is It

What Time Is It?

The clock shows 3 o'clock.

What Time Is It?

The clock shows 3:30.

What Time Is It?

The clock shows 4 o'clock.

What Time Is It?

The clock shows 4:30.

What Time Is It

5:30

What Time Is It?

The clock shows 5 o'clock.

5:00

What Time Is It?

The clock shows 5:30.

6:30

What Time Is It?

The clock shows 6 o'clock.

6:00

What Time Is It?

The clock shows 6:30.

What Time Is It

7:00

What Time Is It?

The clock shows 7 o'clock.

7:30

What Time Is It?

The clock shows 7:30.

8:00

What Time Is It?

The clock shows 8 o'clock.

8:30

What Time Is It?

The clock shows 8:30.

What Time Is It

9:30

What Time Is It?

The clock shows 9:30.

9:00

What Time Is It?

The clock shows 9 o'clock.

10:30

What Time Is It?

The clock shows 10 o'clock.

10:00

What Time Is It?

The clock shows 10:30.

What Time Is It

What Time Is It?

The clock shows 11 o'clock.

What Time Is It?

The clock shows 11:30.

What Time Is It?

The clock shows 12 o'clock.

What Time Is It?

The clock shows 12:30.

Every sentence must start with a capital letter and end with proper punctuation. Capital Letters: An uppercase letter usually bigger than other letters in a word.

Directions: Write the small, a - z sentences, on the lines provided using proper punctuation and capitalization. Most sentences end with a period (.) which is used when a statement is made. The first one is done for you.

i ate an apple A *I ate an apple.*

i buy books B _____

i can cook C _____

i dig down in the dirt D _____

i eat eggs E _____

i feed frogs F _____

i got new glasses today G _____

i have a house H _____

ice is in the igloo I _____

jean jackets are cool J _____

kids love kites K _____

lions live long L _____

my mouth is moving M _____

175

Every sentence must start with a capital letter and end with proper punctuation. Capital Letters: An uppercase letter usually bigger than other letters in a word.

Directions: Write the small, a - z sentences, on the lines provided using proper punctuation and capitalization. Most sentences end with a period (.) which is used when a statement is made. The first one is done for you.

no good news N *No good news.*

on or off O _____

pie in a pan P _____

the queen is quiet Q _____

rhyme or reason R _____

see and say S _____

the time is ticking T _____

under the umbrella U _____

vowels are easy V _____

when or why W _____

x-ray my bones X _____

you are young Y _____

zilch means zero Z _____

WORDS YOUR KINDERGARTNER AND FIRST GRADER SHOULD KNOW

bay	rage	bow	beef	band	doll	mine
day	damp	low	beet	hand	game	ours
hay	lamp	mow	feet	land	toy	the
may	stamp	tow	meet	cube	train	they
pay	bow	crow	beep	tube	get	them
ray	how	stow	deep	eat	got	him
say	now	all	jeep	heat	say	her
way	cow	ball	peep	meat	said	it
fray	wow	call	bell	seat	car	bowl
gray	here	fall	fell	dust	bus	fork
play	there	hall	well	gust	boat	spoon
pray	tie	mall	book	must	best	home
stray	pie	tall	cook	rust	pest	lawn
bake	lie	wall	took	law	rest	mall
cake	die	ask	bold	paw	test	pond
fake	bike	bask	cold	raw	west	room
lake	dike	mask	fold	saw	hide	zoo
make	hike	task	hold	find	ride	
take	like	had	mold	hind	wide	
ate	pike	Have	sold	kind	bump	
date	by	as	told	mind	dump	
fate	cry	if	cone	cat	hump	
gate	dry	in	bone	cow	lump	
hate	fry	is	one	bird	pump	
late	try	with	two	deer	mom	
mate	toe	bent	three	dog	baby	
rate	hoe	dent	four	duck	girl	
age	paw	lent	five	frog	boy	
cage	raw	tent	six	lion	his	
page	saw	bee	and	ball	her	

177

WORDS YOUR FIRST GRADER SHOULD KNOW

add	bring	cool	every	golf	inside	meet
after	brook	corn	fang	gone	into	men
again	brother	could	farther	grape	jaw	mice
any	brown	cram	fast	grass	joke	milk
apart	bush	crew	father	gray	juice	mine
apple	came	crib	fell	green	jump	mint
arm	cane	crow	few	grew	just	mix
baby	card	crowd	field	grit	keep	moon
bake	cart	crown	fill	gull	king	more
bang	case	cube	fine	had	kite	morning
banana	chain	dark	first	hand	know	mother
bark	chair	deal	flag	hang	last	much
beat	chalk	desk	flat	happy	lake	mule
been	chat	dew	flew	hard	late	must
being	chin	dime	flower	harm	like	nail
belt	chop	dine	fog	has	lime	name
bent	clam	dirt	fool	have	line	neat
best	clan	doll	foot	heat	live	neck
bill	clap	door	fort	heavy	look	nest
bike	class	draw	free	help	love	never
bird	claw	dress	fresh	here	luck	next
birth	clay	drink	from	hide	made	new
bone	clean	drop	game	hill	maid	nine
born	clover	dull	gang	hint	make	noon
black	cloud	each	gave	home	many	nose
blew	crayon	east	gift	hope	map	note
block	club	easy	girl	horn	mask	now
blue	coat	eight	give	how	may	odd
book	come	eleven	glad	hush	meal	of
brag	cook	end	going	ill	meat	old

WORDS YOUR FIRST GRADER SHOULD KNOW

once	road	sick	stove	took	which	use
open	rock	side	straw	train	white	used
orange	rode	size	string	trip	who	very
other	room	sled	such	truck	will	vest
over	rope	sleep	summer	trust	wing	vote
pain	round	slip	sun	try	winter	wait
pants	rub	slow	swing	twelve	with	walk
part	rubber	sister	table	thank	woman	want
pave	sail	smell	tail	them	women	was
pear	sale	snail	take	then	yell	water
pen	same	snap	tale	there	zero	well
pencil	sank	snore	tank	think	zone	were
pets	save	snow	team	those	time	west
pick	see	snug	tell	tree	today	when
pink	seed	six	ten	under	took	which
plan	seen	soda	tent	upon	train	white
plant	seep	sofa	test	use	trip	who
play	sell	sold	thank	used	truck	will
poor	send	some	their	very	trust	wing
pretty	seven	soon	them	vest	try	winter
print	shall	spit	then	vote	twelve	with
punch	shape	star	these	wait	thank	woman
purple	sink	start	they	walk	them	women
put	shake	Step	thick	want	then	yell
rain	shirt	stew	thing	was	there	zero
rang	ship	still	think	water	think	zone
rank	shoes	stir	third	well	those	
read	shop	stone	this	were	tree	
ride	show	stool	time	west	under	
river	shut	stop	today	when	upon	

SINGLE DIGIT ADDITION

7	4	0	2	1	8
+2	+3	+9	+5	+8	+2

6	8	7	1	0	5
+0	+1	+3	+7	+4	+2

4	5	9	3	1	7
+0	+3	+1	+4	+7	+2

DOUBLE DIGIT ADDITION WITH NO REGROUPING

PLUS SIGN

14	15	18	13	12
+02	+03	+01	+05	+06

14	15	18	13	12
+02	+03	+01	+05	+06

16	14	11	10	15
+00	+02	+05	+07	+01

SINGLE DIGIT SUBTRACTION

MINUS SIGN

9	1	8	7	2	3
-2	-0	-1	-5	-0	-2

4	5	6	3	9	6
-1	-1	-2	-1	-4	-4

5	8	5	8	9	3
-3	-8	-2	-1	-9	-3

DOUBLE DIGIT SUBTRACTION WITH NO REGROUPING

MINUS SIGN

19	10	18	17	20	13
-10	-00	-11	-15	-00	-12

14	15	16	13	19	16
-04	-04	-05	-02	-14	-03

15	13	12	18	14	11
-03	-02	-02	-10	-03	-10

SINGLE DIGIT ADDITION

Create your own addition math problems and solve them correctly. Use the blank spaces provided below. The first one has been done for you.

```
  1
 +6
 ---
  7
```

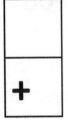 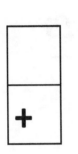 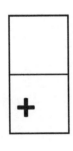 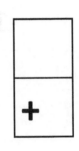  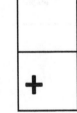

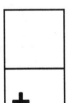 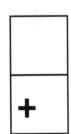  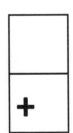 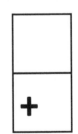  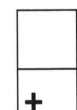

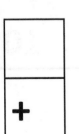 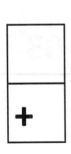 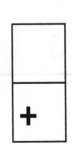 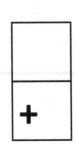 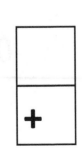  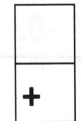

DOUBLE DIGIT ADDITION WITH NO REGROUPING

Create your own addition math problems and solve them correctly. Use the blank spaces provided below. The first one has been done for you.

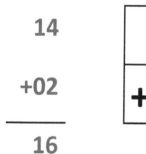 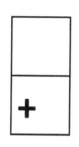 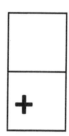 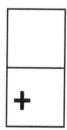 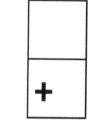

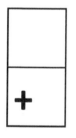 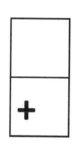 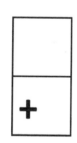 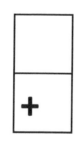 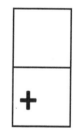 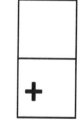

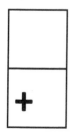 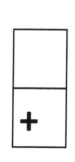 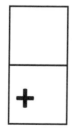 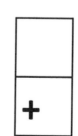 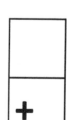 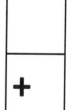

SINGLE DIGIT SUBTRACTION

Create your own subtraction math problems and solve them correctly. Use the blank spaces provided below. The first one has been done for you.

MINUS SIGN

```
  9
 -2
 ---
  7
```

DOUBLE DIGIT SUBTRACTION WITH NO REGROUPING

Create your own subtraction math problems and solve them correctly. Use the blank spaces provided below. The first one has been done for you.

MINUS SIGN

19
-10
___
9

Phonics - For Pre-school thru First Grade

aa baa

ab cab dab jab nab tab

ac Mac sac

ad bad cad dad fad gad had lad mad pad sad tad

ag bag gag hag jag lag nag rag sag tag wag

ah bah hah nah rah Yah

ai jai tai

ak yak

al bal cal gal mal pal

am bam cam dam ham lam ram tam yam

an ban can fan man pan ran tan van wan

ap cap gap hap lap map nap pap rap sap tap yap zap

Phonics - For Pre-school thru First Grade

ar bar car far gar jar mar par tar

as bas das gas has pas vas was

at bat cat fat gat hat lat mat pat rat sat tat vat

aw caw haw jaw law maw raw saw taw yaw

ax fax lax max sax tax wax

ay bay cay day hay jay lay may nay ray say way

ea kea lea mea pea sea tea yea

eb neb web

ec sec

ed bed fed ked led med red Ted wed zed

ee bee fee gee lee nee pee see tee wee zee

ef def ref

Phonics - For Pre-school thru First Grade

ey fey hey key

ez fez

ia via

ib bib dib fib jib lib

ic hic sic tic

id bid fid hid kid lid mid rid

ie die fie lie pie tie

if dif gif

ig big cig dig fig gig jig pig rig wig

il mil nil

im dim him Kim rim Tim vim

in bin din fin gin kin min pin sin tin win yin

io bio

ip dip hip jip kip lip nip pip rip sip tip yip zip

Phonics - For Pre-school thru First Grade

eg beg deg keg leg meg peg

ei lei

el del eel gel

em fem gem hem tem

en den fen hen ken men pen ten yen Zen

eo geo neo

ep pep rep sep yep

er her per ser

es des yes

et bet get jet let met net pet ret set vet wet yet

ev dev rev

ew dew few hew mew new pew sew yew

ex hex rex vex

Phonics - For Pre-school thru First Grade

ir cir dir fir sir

is his sis

it bit cit fit hit kit lit nit pit sit tit wit zit

iv div

ix fix mix nix pix six

iz biz wiz

oa boa moa

ob bob cob fob gob hob job lob mob rob sob

oc doc hoc loc roc soc voc

od cod god mod nod pod rod sod

ua qua

ub cub dub hub nub pub rub sub tub

ud bud cud dud mud

Spelling Word Families - ale

Directions: Write each word in the empty spaces. Study the list for your spelling test.

bale		sale	
dale		scale	
hale		tale	
kale		vale	
male		wale	
pale		whale	

Spelling Word Families - ain

Directions: Write each word in the empty spaces. Study the list for your spelling test.

brain		pain	
chain		plain	
drain		rain	
gain		stain	
grain		strain	
main		train	

Spelling Word Families - ad

Directions: Write each word in the empty spaces. Study the list for your spelling test.

bad		lad	
cad		mad	
dad		pad	
fad		rad	
glad		sad	
grad		tad	
had			

Spelling Word Families - ack

Directions: Write each word in the empty spaces. Study the list for your spelling test.

back		sack	
black		snack	
crack		stack	
pack		tack	
quack		track	
rack		whack	

Spelling Word Families - est

Directions: Write each word in the empty spaces. Study the list for your spelling test.

best		pest	
blest		quest	
chest		rest	
crest		test	
jest		vest	
lest		west	
nest		zest	

Spelling Word Families - ent

Directions: Write each word in the empty spaces. Study the list for your spelling test.

bent		rent	
cent		scent	
dent		sent	
event		spent	
gent		tent	
lent		vent	
pent		went	

Spelling Word Families - eep

Directions: Write each word in the empty spaces. Study the list for your spelling test.

beep

jeep

keep

deep

sheep

sleep

peep

sweep

Name_____

Word Play

Write and spell untaught words phonetically by changing the beginning letter for each word. The first one has been done for you.

ban	*cap*	___ar	___at
___an	___ap	___ar	___at
___an	___ap	___ar	___at
___an	___ap	___ar	___at
___an	___ap	___ar	___at
___an	___ap	___ar	___at
___an	___ap	___ar	___at
___an	___ap	___ar	___at
___an	___ap	___ar	___at
___an	___ap	___ar	___at

Name_____

Word Play

Write and spell untaught words phonetically by changing the beginning letter for each word. The first one has been done for you.

big	*dim*	____in	____ip
____ig	____im	____in	____ip
____ig	____im	____in	____ip
____ig	____im	____in	____ip
____ig	____im	____in	____ip
____ig	____im	____in	____ip
____ig	____im	____in	____ip
____ig	____im	____in	____ip
____ig	____im	____in	____ip
____ig	____im	____in	____ip

Name_____

Prepositions

Prepositions: Words that introduce information to the reader that are short and usually stand in front of nouns. Write your own small sentences using the prepositions *on, in, or to.*

Examples: Class starts <u>on</u> Monday. We have lunch <u>in</u> an hour. From me <u>to</u> you.

1. _____
2. _____
3. _____
4. _____
5. _____
6. _____
7. _____
8. _____
9. _____

Name_____

Conjunctions

Conjunctions: A word that joins other words, phrases, or clauses. The most common ones are and, or, and but. Write your own small sentences using the conjunctions *or, and, or but.*

Example: I like apples <u>and</u> grapes.

1. _____
2. _____
3. _____
4. _____
5. _____
6. _____
7. _____
8. _____
9. _____

Name_____

Show an Opinion

Being able to express an opinion or thought is very important. Finish the sentences that were started by inserting your own opinion or choice.
Examples: My favorite book is <u>Leo the Lop.</u>

1. My favorite toy is _____.

2. I think the color_____ is the best color of all.

3. _____ is my favorite season.

4. I think _____ is the best time of day.

5. My favorite fruit is _____.

6. My favorite vegetable is _____.

7. I wish I was _____ years old.

Practice Writing Sheets
My name, address, and phone number.

Name_____

Writing Your Own Name

Use the lines below to practice writing your name.

How high can you count? Starting at number 1, try to write up to 100.

1									

1	2	3	4	5	6	7	8	9	10
11	12	13	14	15	16	17	18	19	20
21	22	23	24	25	26	27	28	29	30
31	32	33	34	35	36	37	38	39	40
41	42	43	44	45	46	47	48	49	50
51	52	53	54	55	56	57	58	59	60
61	62	63	64	65	66	67	68	69	70
71	72	73	74	75	76	77	78	79	80
81	82	83	84	85	86	87	88	89	90
91	92	93	94	95	96	97	98	99	100

Name_____

Paleo Hebrew Alphabet

Practice writing the Paleo Hebrew alphabet or symbol.

Paleo Hebrew
Alphabet Worksheets

Name_____

Paleo Hebrew Alphabet

Practice writing the Paleo Hebrew alphabet or symbol.

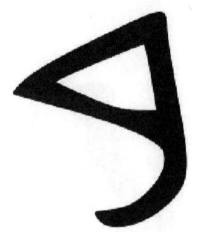   B

ʒ ---------------------------------------

Paleo Hebrew
Alphabet Worksheets

Name_____

Paleo Hebrew Alphabet

Practice writing the Paleo Hebrew alphabet or symbol.

Paleo Hebrew
Alphabet Worksheets

Name_____

Paleo Hebrew Alphabet

Practice writing the Paleo Hebrew alphabet or symbol.

Paleo Hebrew
Alphabet Worksheets

Name_____

Paleo Hebrew Alphabet

Practice writing the Paleo Hebrew alphabet or symbol.

Paleo Hebrew
Alphabet Worksheets

213

Name_____

Paleo Hebrew Alphabet

Practice writing the Paleo Hebrew alphabet or symbol.

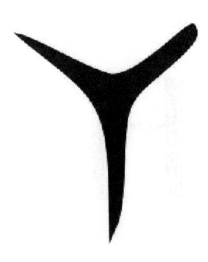 

Paleo Hebrew Alphabet Worksheets

Name_____

Paleo Hebrew Alphabet

Practice writing the Paleo Hebrew alphabet or symbol.

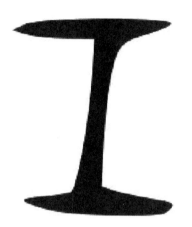 z

I

Paleo Hebrew
Alphabet Worksheets

215

Name_____

Paleo Hebrew Alphabet

Practice writing the Paleo Hebrew alphabet or symbol.

Paleo Hebrew
Alphabet Worksheets

Name_____

Paleo Hebrew Alphabet

Practice writing the Paleo Hebrew alphabet or symbol.

Paleo Hebrew
Alphabet Worksheets

Name_____

Paleo Hebrew Alphabet

Practice writing the Paleo Hebrew alphabet or symbol.

Paleo Hebrew
Alphabet Worksheets

Name_____

Paleo Hebrew Alphabet

Practice writing the Paleo Hebrew alphabet or symbol.

Paleo Hebrew
Alphabet Worksheets

Name_____

Paleo Hebrew Alphabet

Practice writing the Paleo Hebrew alphabet or symbol.

Paleo Hebrew
Alphabet Worksheets

Name_____

Paleo Hebrew Alphabet

Practice writing the Paleo Hebrew alphabet or symbol.

Paleo Hebrew
Alphabet Worksheets

Name_____

Paleo Hebrew Alphabet

Practice writing the Paleo Hebrew alphabet or symbol.

Paleo Hebrew Alphabet Worksheets

222

Name_____

Paleo Hebrew Alphabet

Practice writing the Paleo Hebrew alphabet or symbol.

 S

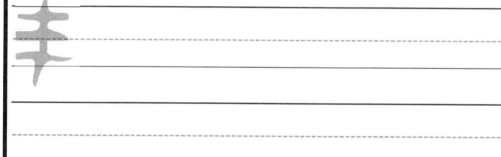

Paleo Hebrew
Alphabet Worksheets

Name_____

Paleo Hebrew Alphabet

Practice writing the Paleo Hebrew alphabet or symbol.

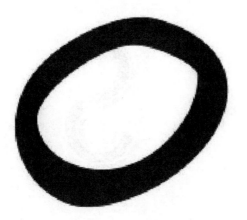

Paleo Hebrew
Alphabet Worksheets

Name_____

Paleo Hebrew Alphabet

Practice writing the Paleo Hebrew alphabet or symbol.

Paleo Hebrew
Alphabet Worksheets

Name_____

Paleo Hebrew Alphabet

Practice writing the Paleo Hebrew alphabet or symbol.

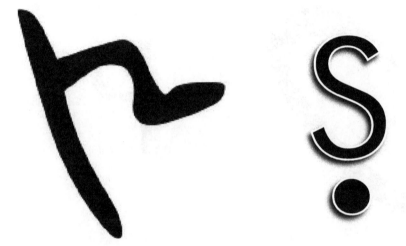

Paleo Hebrew
Alphabet Worksheets

226

Name_____

Paleo Hebrew Alphabet

Practice writing the Paleo Hebrew alphabet or symbol.

Paleo Hebrew
Alphabet Worksheets

227

Name_____

Paleo Hebrew Alphabet

Practice writing the Paleo Hebrew alphabet or symbol.

Paleo Hebrew
Alphabet Worksheets

Name_____

Paleo Hebrew Alphabet

Practice writing the Paleo Hebrew alphabet or symbol.

Paleo Hebrew
Alphabet Worksheets

Name_____

Paleo Hebrew Alphabet

Practice writing the Paleo Hebrew alphabet or symbol.

T

Paleo Hebrew
Alphabet Worksheets

230

Name_____

Paleo Hebrew Alphabet

Practice writing the Paleo Hebrew name Yahuah

Yahuah, in Paleo Hebrew

Paleo Hebrew Worksheets

Name_____

Paleo Hebrew Alphabet

Practice writing the Paleo Hebrew name Yah

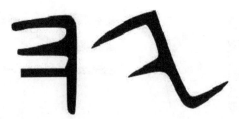

Yah, in Paleo Hebrew

Paleo Hebrew
Worksheets

Name_____

The Sons of Jacob (Yisrael)

Practice writing the information for knowledge.

Reuben (*Re'uven*) - 1st born son
Leah is his mother.

12 TRIBES OF ISRAEL
Worksheets

Name_____

The Sons of Jacob (Yisrael)

Practice writing the information for knowledge.

Simeon (Shim'on) - 2nd born son
Leah is his mother.

12 TRIBES OF ISRAEL
Worksheets

Name_____

The Sons of Jacob (Yisrael)

Practice writing the information for knowledge.

Levi (Leviy) - 3rd born son
Leah is his mother.

_____
- - - - - - - - - - - - - - - - - - -
_____

_____
- - - - - - - - - - - - - - - - - - -
_____

_____
- - - - - - - - - - - - - - - - - - -
_____

_____
- - - - - - - - - - - - - - - - - - -
_____

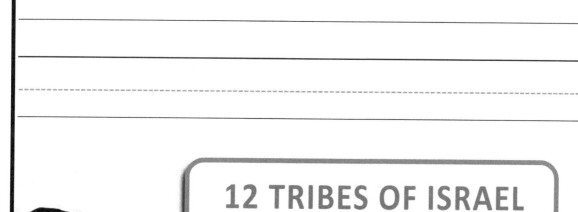

12 TRIBES OF ISRAEL
Worksheets

Name_____

The Sons of Jacob (Yisrael)

Practice writing the information for knowledge.

Judah (Yahudah) - 4th born son
Leah is his mother.

12 TRIBES OF ISRAEL
Worksheets

Name_____

The Sons of Jacob (Yisrael)

Practice writing the information for knowledge.

Dan - 5th born son
Bilhah is his mother.

12 TRIBES OF ISRAEL
Worksheets

Name_____

The Sons of Jacob (Yisrael)

Practice writing the information for knowledge.

Naphtali (Naphtaliy) - 6th born son
Bilhah is his mother.

12 TRIBES OF ISRAEL
Worksheets

Name_____

The Sons of Jacob (Yisrael)

Practice writing the information for knowledge.

Gad - 7th born son
Zilpah is his mother.

12 TRIBES OF ISRAEL
Worksheets

Name_____

The Sons of Jacob (Yisrael)

Practice writing the information for knowledge.

Asher - 8th born son
Zilpah is his mother.

12 TRIBES OF ISRAEL
Worksheets

Name_____

The Sons of Jacob (Yisrael)

Practice writing the information for knowledge.

Issachar (Yissaskar) - 9th born son
Leah is his mother.

Name_____

The Sons of Jacob (Yisrael)

Practice writing the information for knowledge.

Zebulun (Zevulun) - 10th born son
Leah is his mother.

12 TRIBES OF ISRAEL
Worksheets

Name_____

The Sons of Jacob (Yisrael)

Practice writing the information for knowledge.

Joseph (Yoceph) - 11th born son
Rachel is his mother.

12 TRIBES OF ISRAEL
Worksheets

Name_____

The Sons of Jacob (Yisrael)

Practice writing the information for knowledge.

Benjamin (Binyamiyn) - 12th born son
Rachel is his mother.

12 TRIBES OF ISRAEL
Worksheets

HEBREW TERMS FOR KINSHIPS

Directions: Use the space beside each kinship word to practice writing the *Hebrew Words*.

Family - Mishpacha	
Dad - Abba	
Mom - Ima	
Brother - Ach	
Sister - Achot	
Son - Ben	
Daughter - Bat (Baht)	
Grandpa - Saba/Sabba	
Grandma - Savta/Safta	
Uncle - Dod	
Aunt - Dodah	
Male Cousin - Ben Dod	
Female Cousin - Bat/Bas Dodah	
Nephew - Ahkh Yahn	
Niece - Ahkh Yah Neet	
Hello Friend - Alo Haver	
Male Friend - Chaver	
Female Friend - Chaverah	

Directions: Use five of the *Hebrew Words* in a sentence on the lines provided below.

1. _____

2. _____

3. _____

4. _____

5. _____

HEBREW TERMS FOR KINSHIPS
Ima = Mom

Directions: Use the lines below to write sentences using the Hebrew term for the above word. An example has been done for you.

(My Ima is very nice.)

1. _____

2. _____

3. _____

4. _____

5. _____

Abba = Dad

Directions: Use the lines below to write sentences using the Hebrew term for the above word. An example has been done for you.

(My abba loves reading.)

1. _____

2. _____

3. _____

4. _____

5. _____

HEBREW TERMS FOR KINSHIPS
Ach = Brother

Directions: Use the lines below to write sentences using the Hebrew term for the above word. An example has been done for you.

(My ach is always taking my toys.)

1. _____

2. _____

3. _____

4. _____

5. _____

Achot = Sister

Directions: Use the lines below to write sentences using the Hebrew term for the above word. An example has been done for you.

(My achot is my best friend.)

1. _____

2. _____

3. _____

4. _____

5. _____

HEBREW TERMS FOR KINSHIPS

Sabba = Grandpa

Directions: Use the lines below to write sentences using the Hebrew term for the above word. An example has been done for you.

(My sabba is very funny.)

1. _____

2. _____

3. _____

4. _____

5. _____

Safta = Grandma

Directions: Use the lines below to write sentences using the Hebrew term for the above word. An example has been done for you.

(My safta made cookies yesterday.)

1. _____

2. _____

3. _____

4. _____

5. _____

HEBREW TERMS FOR KINSHIPS

Ben = Son

Directions: Use the lines below to write sentences using the Hebrew term for the above word. An example has been done for you.

(I am the third ben born to my parents.)

1. _____

2. _____

3. _____

4. _____

5. _____

Bat (Baht) = Daughter

Directions: Use the lines below to write sentences using the Hebrew term for the above word. An example has been done for you.

(My mom says I'm her funniest Bat.)

1. _____

2. _____

3. _____

4. _____

5. _____

HEBREW TERMS FOR KINSHIPS
Mishpacha = Family

Directions: Use the lines below to write sentences using the Hebrew term for the above word. An example has been done for you.

(Our mishpacha went to the park yesterday.)

1. _____

2. _____

3. _____

4. _____

5. _____

Alo Haver = Hello Friend

Directions: Use the lines below to write sentences using the Hebrew term for the above word. An example has been done for you.

(Every morning, Rebecca says, alo haver to me.)

1. _____

2. _____

3. _____

4. _____

5. _____